D0961724

The Job Survival Instruction Book,

Third Edition: 400+ Tips, Tricks, and Techniques to Stay Employed

Karin Ireland

Course Technology PTR

A part of Cengage Learning

COURSE TECHNOLOGY
CENGAGE Learning

Australia, Brazil, Japan, Korea, Mexico, Singapore, Spain, United Kingdom, United States

For product information and technology assistance, contact us at
Cengage Learning Academic Resource Center, 1-800-354-9706

For permission to use material from this text or product,
submit all requests online at **cengage.com/permissions**
Further permissions questions can be emailed to
permissionrequest@cengage.com

Library of Congress Catalog Card Number: 2009941739

ISBN-13: 978-1-4354-5710-2

ISBN-10: 1-4354-5710-2

Course Technology, a part of Cengage Learning
20 Channel Center Street, Boston, MA 02210, USA

Cengage Learning is a leading provider of customized learning solutions with office locations around the globe, including Singapore, the United Kingdom, Australia, Mexico, Brazil, and Japan. Locate your local office at:
international.cengage.com/region

Cengage Learning products are represented in Canada by Nelson Education, Ltd.
For your lifelong learning solutions, visit **courseptr.com**
Visit our corporate website at **cengage.com**

Printed in the United States of America
2 3 4 5 6 7 12 11 10

For Francis, who always believes in me, and for Tricia, who lived through my learning this.

Karin Ireland has been a writer for more years than she'd like to admit, and spent many of them working for other people. She passes along what she learned the hard way, and hopes you will be quicker to balance who you are with what you do, so you'll have a smoother journey.

Nothing is impossible with the right attitude
and an endless amount of chocolate.

Accept competition when it excites you; avoid
competition when it causes you to feel anxious
or angry.

When you're asked to do something you don't
know how to do, don't panic. Nod confidently,
leave calmly, and find someone who does know
how to do it.

Perfection is relative. Perfect for some tasks is creating an award-winning masterpiece. Perfect for others is just getting the job done.

Be decisive when you speak. Decisive people receive more attention and respect, even when they're wrong, than people who are right but sound uncertain.

The three most important parts of your job performance are attitude, attitude, and attitude.

Instead of crafting your resume to reflect what you want the interviewer to know about you, craft it to meet their needs. Make your resume show not only the skills you have that the company needs, but also how you are exactly who they want.

A new boss means new rules. It's like switching from baseball to football. Meet the challenge of playing the new game instead of struggling to play a new game with the old rules.

Take inventory often: Is what you're doing getting you where you want to go at work? Is your job getting you where you want to go in *life?*

Go to meetings prepared and on time.

Consider your quality of life when evaluating your job. Many men have worked days, nights, and weekends to provide security for their family only to have their wives leave them because they were never home.

Prioritize your work according to the 80/20 rule: Do the 20 percent that gives you 80 percent of the results.

Don't necessarily believe the interviewer when she says the company values innovative employees who speak up. See how employees who speak up are treated before you speak up too loudly.

When you're really sick, stay home. Nobody wants to catch what you've got.

Think before you ask questions; ask questions before you guess.

Specialize in something at work and be the best. *Someone* will, and you'll have more fun if it's you.

People have different styles of communicating —even in their emails. Respond to emails from your boss and coworkers in the style they write to you.

Establish personal boundaries that are comfortable for you and then gently, politely, but firmly, request that others honor them.

When your boss comes to visit, put your pen or pencil down and be attentive.

When you write, keep it simple. Keep it focused. Keep it as short as it can be and still be complete.

Do the best you can, then leave work and forget about it.

Say what you mean.
Mean what you say.
Do what you say you will do.

When the going gets tough, keep breathing.
Deep, rhythmic breathing. Relax your jaw and
shoulders, and imagine you're on a tropical beach.

Don't make a habit of working overtime.
After a while, it will be expected, and what
you're able to do in a crunch will become
what you're expected to do every day.

Don't put up with an intolerable situation.
When you say, *yes, but...*, you close the door
to looking for solutions. Instead of saying, *yes,
but...*, look for solutions.

Understand what your boss wants you to do
and then, if you can, do it.

No one feels confident or competent all the
time. Fake it till you make it. Others will
believe you're successful and, pretty soon, you
will, too.

An interviewer who seems almost like a friend is not your friend. Her job is to weed out people who might not fit or might be a problem in the company. Many personal questions are illegal for interviewers to ask, but they can engage you in friendly conversation hoping you might share that information voluntarily.

When you find yourself rehashing failures, mentally erase the scene and think of some successes instead.

When people praise you for your brilliance, don't argue that you aren't. Simply smile, thank them, and be quiet.

Know the names and faces of your company's top executives.

Your relationship with your supervisor can be a big part of your job satisfaction. Try to choose a good boss over great pay.

Learn the fine art of saying little about things you know nothing about.

Don't email or Twitter something you wouldn't want passed around. Don't post anything negative about your job or anyone you work with on your social network.

Meet deadlines by marking your calendar with each due date. Estimate how long each part of the project will take and move backward on the calendar to set up a schedule.

Know if it's okay to use your cell phone, text, Twitter, or check your personal email at work, and if it isn't, don't. Know your company's policy on personal use of the copy and fax machine and follow it.

Prescription for workaholics: Do one less task a day than you think you have to or can.

Always tell the truth (but not necessarily all of it).

What goes around comes around. Keep that in mind, or be ready to duck.

When you aren't sure what to do, don't do anything until you ask or figure it out.

Don't just wish things were different. Figure out exactly what you want, then look for ways to make that happen.

Management that doesn't have the time or money to do a job the way workers say it should be done will find time and money to redo it when they discover the workers were right. Take a deep breath, and let it go.

Anger that's hidden always comes out—usually at inappropriate times. Learn to communicate anger appropriately or let it go.

Never assume it's okay to swear, even if others do.

Three strategies for successful negotiation:

- ✽ Work to achieve your goal rather than to defend your position.

- ✽ Stick to the subject.

- ✽ Look for solutions where everyone wins.

Respond to the person, not the gestures, accents, or habits that remind you of someone else.

Never assume you know who the group leader is. Address everyone the same until the leader indicates he or she is who you should address.

Courtesy always counts.

Think of your job as a game that you've agreed to play. Play the position you were hired to play; don't expect to agree with the referee or even the coach all the time. Do your best, and then go home and do something else.

Set your watch ahead four minutes and forget you did it. You'll be surprised how much more often you arrive at work and meetings on time.

When someone resists your ideas, ask questions before you try to explain the resistance away.

Whatever you believe, you achieve. With this law, you create both what you want and what you don't want.

Pursue balance in everything. Even in pursuing balance.

Don't feel you have to reinvent the wheel. When you're under deadline pressure, getting the job done is usually more important than finding a new or better way to do it.

Accept ownership for your good ideas—or others will.

When your boss suggests a change, agree to try it. If it doesn't work, you can always suggest going back to the old way.

When you make a complaint, know the resolution you want and ask for it.

The more you try to be in control, the less you really are...in life and at work.

Assertiveness is relative. Learn what's acceptable for each person and group, and adjust your approach accordingly.

Never say anything at work you wouldn't want your coworkers and boss to hear.

Develop a good relationship with your superiors. Get to know what they want and need from you and then give it to them. You will have more opportunities and more support if they know and trust you.

· Confirm appointments before you leave your office.

Create an extra work break by switching from one project to another. Take a few deep breaths after putting one project aside before starting the other.

It's tempting to leave folders on your desk so you don't forget about them, but it can also seem overwhelming. Instead, make a list of your projects, and put the folders in a "to do" file. Consult your list every day to make sure nothing gets overlooked.

Four words to eliminate:

- ✳ should
- ✳ shouldn't
- ✳ can't
- ✳ try

Quit smoking.

Do willingly the tasks your boss has the power and inclination to make you do.

Don't believe everything you hear.
Don't believe everything you see.
Don't believe everything you're promised.

Employees who are helpful and easy to get
along with are often valued more than difficult
people with better skills. Make your boss glad
he hired you.

Excuses don't matter. What matters are results.

Timing is important. Approach your boss when you know she will be receptive.

Listen to the grapevine; it's usually at least partly right. Be discriminating about what you pass along.

Quit gracefully. When you're ready to leave, tell your boss in person, *then* send a written resignation letter. Thank him for the support you've received and for the opportunities to learn whatever you learned. Leave on a positive note. Do not tell your boss what's wrong with the company, management, or your coworkers. If your name ever comes up in the future, you want him to remember you kindly.

If you're a manager and you ask your staff to do something, make sure they do it. If you "forget," or if you do it yourself, you're sending messages to them that they won't be held accountable.

Respond, don't react, to people and situations.

Be willing to compromise on what you do and how you do it, but never compromise on what you believe and who you are. If you can't do your job with integrity, find a new job.

Remember that you come first in your life.
Also, remember that not everyone will share
that view.

Suppress the urge to confess your weaknesses.
Confession doesn't make you look humble; it
just makes you look weak.

If your voice mail promises you'll get back to
callers, do it.

Don't be fooled by a party atmosphere.
Company get-togethers are not the place to
relax and say what you really think of the
company health plan, your workload, or your
boss's new haircut.

Someone said that to be a success, you have to
be different. Look for ways to be different that
benefit you *and* your employer.

Prepare for even the shortest presentation.
Jot down three main points, two supporting
sub-points, and a conclusion or request for
action.

Discourage drop-in visitors from staying by keeping file folders on your chairs.

If you wonder where your time goes, keep a log for a week.

Five ways to appear more professional:

※ Eliminate "uh," "um," "you know," and other fillers from your speech.

※ Talk positively.

※ Develop a firm speaking voice.

※ Don't make your statements sound like a question?

※ Don't get carried away with piercings and tattoos that show.

Don't borrow money from your coworkers.
Don't borrow money from your boss.
Don't lend money to either.

Ask a good friend to let you know if you have
bad breath. If you do, carry breath mints or
consult a dentist.

If a project seems overwhelming, break it into
several steps. Reward yourself each time you
complete a step.

Accept the fact that when you wear your white suit or your best silk tie to work, it will be the day your lunch friends want to go out for spaghetti.

Think of your resume as your first job assignment for each company you apply to. Interviewers won't see your potential; they'll only see what you show them.

If your company is "reorganized," don't assume your responsibilities are the same. If your boss doesn't tell you, ask.

Look for ways a job can be done instead of reasons why it can't.

Never complain about your boss to your coworkers. Never ever complain about your boss to someone in another department. And never complain about your boss to your boss.

Before you leave work, have a clear idea of what you want to accomplish the next day and what you'll do first.

It's less important to get everything done than it is to get the most important things done.

Celebrate the differences between people.

Don't plan your wedding, open house, vacation, or best friend's baby shower on company time. Coworkers hate hearing you have time to plan something fun while they're struggling to get the work done.

Commit 100 percent to what you're doing each moment.

Notice the silent conversations you have with yourself. Make them positive. What you say and think determines how you feel. How you feel determines what you do. What you do determines what you have.

Don't turn small assignments into large projects. Don't make big changes to any project without checking with your boss first. A great idea won't seem great if it causes your boss or someone on your team more work or embarrassment.

Don't interrupt someone you're trying to impress. The longer they talk, the more comfortable they get.

When someone asks how you are, unless it's your mother or your therapist, just say, "Great."

Keep a victory log and write down every time you meet a goal, keep a commitment, or find a win-win solution to a problem.

Never involve yourself in office politics that
don't feel honest to you.

You might be able to take a lower-paying job
you love by lowering your expenses. Buy a
cheaper car or see if you can get by with just
one for your family, shop resale shops, use
coupons. Let go of your "need" for stuff.

Before you do anything, know your goal.
Before you start a project, make a phone call, ask
a question, write a memo, or make a decision—
know the result you want or need, then determine
what you need to do to get it.

If your business call is to someone at home, identify yourself if a family member answers the phone.

Do a good job whether or not someone is looking.

When talking to your boss, stick to the point; be pleasant, but brief.

Do what it takes to show up at work on time.

Don't give your presentation right before lunch or quitting time. People won't really be paying attention.

Make an arrangement with a coworker to signal you when you have green food stuck in your teeth or clothes tags flapping in the breeze.

If you have a bad day at work, do something to break that mood before you go home to your family. Listen to some nice music, eat chocolate, go shopping, meditate, eat chocolate, take a walk, or eat chocolate.

Show respect for your fellow workers, whether or not they deserve it.

Avoid fighting other people's battles. It may feel noble, but it won't make your boss a fan of yours.

When you reward employees and customers, give them something they want, not something you think they should want.

Ask yourself what you can learn from people and situations at work that bother you.

Change happens. It isn't always for the best, but employees who accept it without complaining are appreciated and sometimes even rewarded.

Four strategies for surviving change:

- ❋ Cooperate with whoever is in charge.

- ❋ Appear positive and optimistic.

- ❋ Learn about the goals of those in charge.

- ❋ Do what you can to help them reach those goals.

Accept that if your boss thinks something is important, it is. Being known as a team player is often more valuable than being known as brilliant.

There are no guarantees at work. If you knew your job was on the line, what would you do differently? Do it now.

Take your rest breaks, and don't talk about work. (If you talk about work, it's not a break.)

The best time to hold meetings is midmorning. The worst days are Mondays and Fridays.

It takes just as much energy to be nasty as it takes to be nice. Nasty may feel better at times, but nice will get you farther.

Always keep your resume updated.

Be careful what you wish for; you just might get it.

You can always decide to go back and say something to a boss, coworker, or employee later, but you can never *unsay* something you said.

Be patient with everybody—including yourself.

Begin conflict resolution by asking what the other person thinks before saying what you think. After she's said what's on her mind, she'll be more likely to listen to you.

Do the work you love. If you can't, do what you love as a hobby or volunteer. You may get a job in that area by being at the right place at the right time.

Notice what are facts and what are assumptions. Question some facts and all assumptions.

If you don't ask for something, you'll never know if you could have gotten it.

Five more ways to appear more professional:

- Notice and eliminate nervous habits.

- Dress as nicely as you can afford to.

- Act confident (even if you aren't).

- Look people in the eye.

- Play by your boss's and your company's rules.

Interrupt conversations with co-workers immediately to help customers and clients.

Always have neat, clean fingernails. Fix chipped polish.

If you're with another customer and can't help a new arrival immediately, smile and let her know you'll be right with her. Generally, people are willing to wait. What they're not willing to do is be ignored.

In a power struggle between you and your boss, you will lose. Even if you win, ultimately, you will lose.

Anytime you argue with a customer, you lose. Even if you win, you lose.

When someone thanks you, say, "You're welcome," not "No problem."

People can generally recognize when you're in a bad mood, but they appreciate a warning before you snap.

Information is power. Learn how and where people get it in your company.

When you promise to call someone back with more information, ask when a good time would be to call. It can save both of you many rounds of telephone tag.

You can save time if you limit the number of times you check your emails and limit the length of your responses.

Your ability to cooperate, to keep your boss informed and happy, will be a big part of your performance appraisal.

Use your best manners at meals. Even if you're just with coworkers.

Don't take yourself too seriously. Don't confuse what you do at work with who you are. Deferring to your bosses' preference doesn't make you weak, and it doesn't mean your idea wasn't better; it means your boss will not see you as a troublemaker.

Never ridicule anyone, even as a joke, even to make a point, even if he or she laughs, too.

Don't try to change the system unless it's discriminatory or dangerous. It was there before you were, and something is keeping it there. Instead, learn how to make it work for you, or find a new job.

Most people will treat you the way you expect to be treated.

Know your goals: To do, to have, to be. Review them regularly. Say them out loud for the best results. Visualize yourself already having reached your goals. Feel the satisfaction.

Bosses never quite get their thoughts in order until after you've presented the final draft. Accept this or it will make you crazy.

Question authority, but question it to yourself until you have some authority.

The Golden Rule is still a good idea.

If you need to call someone who is long-winded, begin by saying, "I've only got a second to talk…" and then briefly explain what you need.

Ask yourself often: Am I being productive or just active?

It's usually easier to go *around* a barrier than through it.

When you want something done, go directly to the person who can get it done. (Unless that means going over your boss's head. In that case, look for a way to make your boss think it's his idea; then he'll go to the person who can get it done.)

Waiting until everything is lined up before making a move is like waiting to start a trip until all the traffic lights are green.

Be the kind of person others enjoy having around.

Always listen with the possibility that the person who's talking could be right. Even when you're dead sure he or she is wrong.

Try not to be sick on Fridays or Mondays. No one will believe you.

If you leave voice mail, be discreet. Even though you're invited to leave a "private message," it might not be.

Responding to voice mail by email is often more efficient for you and the caller.

Even though you erase an email, it can still be found. Be careful what you write.

Don't appear desperate at a job interview.

Acknowledge people, especially your boss, quickly when they enter your workspace.

Comparing yourself or your work to other people is a no-win exercise. Compare yourself only to your own best.

Never be late to a job interview. If you absolutely can't help it, apologize simply and have a really good excuse.

Know the difference between an idea and a plan. An idea is simple; a plan requires knowing how the idea will work.

Decide to be happy each day.

Congratulate yourself every day for five things you did well. Little things count as much as big things.

In communication, listening is generally more important than talking.

If you believe you're a victim of sexual, racial, age, or religious discrimination or abuse, tell your boss. If he or she is unwilling or unable to help, tell the next person up the line of command.

Laws protect minority and disabled employees. Help make the world a place where these laws aren't needed.

Set up five daily goals. Carry over what you don't finish to the next day.

Don't make promises you can't keep.

Write memos with real words. Instead of writing, "I have come to the realization that, at the present time, I am unable to give consideration to your request for a job," write this: "At the time, there are no job openings."

Eliminate negative body language that can make you look uncooperative: tapping fingers, rolling eyes, arms locked across the chest, looking away from the speaker, clenched teeth, fidgeting.

When making decisions, weigh the facts; then pay attention to your gut feeling.

Be organized. Write things down. Make to-do lists, schedule meetings, calendar deadlines, and document papers you send and receive.

Four tips for answering the phone:

- ✳ Sound happy to receive the call.

- ✳ Don't challenge callers to give more information than they want to.

- ✳ Don't sound suspicious or bored.

- ✳ Write down the caller's name the first time you hear it.

Join Toastmasters. You'll learn how to speak in front of others and, as Toastmasters says, the butterflies might not go away, but you'll learn how to make them fly in formation.

In order to get the answers you need, you have to ask the right questions.

The perfect job is something you'd do even if nobody paid you.

Show up with donuts for the gang occasionally. Don't do it regularly, though, or people will resent it when you don't.

Keep at least three months' salary in a savings account. Life is uncertain, and if you lose your job, it could take awhile to find another one.

Generally, you can act a little nicer than you feel, but only a *little* nicer. If you try to be a saint, you'll find yourself smiling with clenched teeth.

Most coworkers will be happy to hear your great news or amazing experience. *Once.*

Notice that what you think about and talk about is what shows up in your job and in your life.

Plan something to look forward to each weekend.

Don't expect yourself to be perfect. When you make a mistake, don't make excuses. Just learn from it, and go on.

Be good to every living thing—starting with yourself.

Get a new job offer in writing before you quit your present job or say no to other potential employers.

Avoid "us vs. them" comments or attitudes.

Don't yell at your boss, even if he or she yells at you. It's okay to ask for a break until you both cool down.

Keep learning: Work crossword puzzles, read magazines of your trade, borrow kids' nonfiction books (they're short and to the point) from the library.

Tell coworkers when you hear something good about them.

Don't get so busy *doing* that you forget about *being*—being happy, being patient, being kind.

Don't play "one-upmanship." It's a game without winners.

It isn't enough to be valuable if the right people aren't aware of it. Make yourself noticeable in positive ways.

Let your boss know what you need to succeed, and if you are the boss, provide your employees with what *they* need to succeed.

Nothing can get you as far as good self-esteem.
If you don't have it, learn how to develop it.
If you do have it, work to increase it.

Strive to be curious rather than right.

Don't let things build up. If you have a problem
with a coworker, talk about it and find a solution
that works for both of you.

Partial truth sometimes paints a more accurate
picture than telling all the details.

When people help you, express your thanks
and then surprise them by asking what you can
do for them.

Don't sign anything that isn't exactly true—
even if the person who asks you to sign says
it doesn't mean what it says, that nobody will
hold you to it, or that you can always change
your mind later. If you must sign the document,
cross out the part that troubles you and initial it.

If you're anything less than 100 percent com-
mitted to your present job, keep it to yourself.

Warning: Complaining is habit-forming and
may be hazardous to your health.

Don't let your boss make you feel bad. Do your best and let it go. If you can't, look for another job.

Whenever you think you can't do something, ask yourself this question: If somebody offered you $1 million, would you find a way?

Act—don't react. There's no law that says you have to answer questions or respond to criticisms from your boss or coworkers on the spot. Take time, if you need it, to separate your feelings from the message and then form a response.

Never give anyone the only copy of important paperwork.

Develop a sense of humor. It's better to laugh than to cry, and sometimes those will be your only options.

Work to be good, not perfect.

Avoid office romances. They're distracting when they work and painful when they don't.

Management doesn't always do what is reasonable or fair. Management doesn't appreciate having junior employees tell them that what they're doing isn't reasonable or fair.

Everyone wants to feel special. You can feel special if you help others feel that they are.

People will want you to be perfect. You may believe that you should be perfect. You can't be. But nobody else can, either.

It's usually easier to get forgiveness than it is to get permission.

Being a boss is not a license to be bossy.

Don't interrupt, even when you already know what the other person is going to say and you know that what you have to say is more clever or important.

Four ways to reduce stress:

- ✳ Get some physical exercise every day.

- ✳ Find people to laugh with.

- ✳ Be around people who are positive.

- ✳ Remember to breathe.

Don't share your personal or family struggles at an interview. Employers do not want to hire an employee they think might miss work, be distracted, or quit as soon as he or she's trained.

What you say may not be what the other person hears. What you hear may not be what the other person means. Check it out.

People don't always want advice. Sometimes they only want you to listen and agree that they're right.

At work and in life, you get what you look for.

Get to know the culture of your company by looking at the leaders. The more you appear to be like the leaders, the better your chances are for success.

Give your inner critic a name, and tell it to hush.

Always believe the impossible is possible.

If you make a verbal agreement, it's often a good idea to follow up on the points that were covered—even if it's only in an email. A month down the road, the parties involved may remember a very different conversation.

Life is a journey, not a destination. Be gentle with yourself when you hit bumps in the road. A lot of those bumps will be at work.

Stress buster: Today, only think about things that you need to make a decision on today.

Wear name tags on your right side, where people naturally look when they shake your hand.

Avoid being pledged to secrecy until you have some sense of what the secret is about.

No matter what you do, you won't be able to please everybody all the time. That's okay. Just do your best.

Listening attentively is the most sincere form
of flattery.

Go outside at lunch time, especially if you work
in an air-conditioned office with computer
screens, fluorescent lights, and other unnatural
conditions.

Never doubt that the difficult can be done.

Never disclose information told to you in
confidence—even if you weren't specifically
asked not to tell.

Don't hold an important employee update session on a tight time schedule.

You'll enjoy your job more if you work for the fun things you can do with your money rather than the bills you're going to pay.

Find the right occupation. Find the right company. You'll know when you're there by the way you feel.

Learn the difference between being assertive and being aggressive.

When you're frustrated, ask yourself if it will
matter in 10 years, and if not, take a deep
breath and let it go.

Smile when you dial or answer the phone.
Be as friendly and helpful as if you were
talking to a friend.

If you lead a meeting, begin by stating the
purpose.

If you keep doing things the way you're doing
them now, you'll keep getting the same results.
To see changes in what you get, you need to
change what you do.

Never help someone with the punch line of a joke.
Never help your boss with any part of a joke.

Practice putting yourself in the other person's
shoes.

Everyone is in sales. Learn how to sell yourself,
your ideas, your value.

Demonstrate your power as confidence and
inner calm instead of outward bravado.

Treat people nicely even when there's nothing in it for you.

Don't mumble.
Don't whine.
Don't cheat on your expense reports.

Don't wait to listen to inspiration and motivation tapes till you need them. Listen to them when you're up, and maybe you won't ever feel like you *need* them.

There's an old saying, "Don't shoot the messenger." In job talk, that means don't be angry with your boss if he passes along bad news from *his* boss.

Do the job you were hired to do and then volunteer for other work if you have time.

Put some money in a savings account every payday.

Life is supposed to be fun. If you have a bad day, decide to have a good day tomorrow.

Surround yourself with the brightest, sharpest people you can find. Generally, you're known by the company you keep.

If you're the boss, hire people who are the best for the job, and don't sabotage them if they're smarter than you.

Sandwich criticism between genuine compliments.

Don't let anybody at work know you're looking for another job. If your boss finds out, you might be leaving sooner than you planned.

If you can't explain your idea in a couple of minutes, you probably aren't ready to explain it.

Don't make decisions based on the experiences of others.

Five things job interviewers want to know:

⚜ Why you think you can do the job.

⚜ How well you will fit in with the current staff.

⚜ How skilled you are.

⚜ How willing you are.

⚜ Why you should be chosen over other applicants.

Identify someone at your company who is well-informed and become friends.

If you look for sympathy, you'll probably get it.
Look for answers and you're more likely to
solve the problem.

If may be unfair, but people judge you by the
way you look. Do the best with what you have.

Don't upstage your boss.

Evaluate your behavior/performance regularly
to see if you're on track, but learn to turn off
your internal critic (the voice that tells you you're
not measuring up no matter what you do).

Replace scuffed briefcases, worn or dirty purses, rundown heels. It *does* matter

Replace bad habits with good ones, old skills with updated ones, negative friends with positive ones.

Let other people own their behavior. Don't assume that if your boss, coworker, or client is in a bad mood it's your fault.

Own your own behavior. Don't blame other people for your bad mood.

Attack the problem, not the person.

Be nice to your boss even if you don't like him or her. Ask yourself what you can learn from the situation. If it's intolerable, look for a new job.

Tell the secretary why you're calling the boss— don't play games.

People will respect you more if you let them feel great when they're with you than if you try to convince them how great you are.

Write down three things you'd like to be known for, decide how you can make that happen, and then take action.

When others complain about a coworker, change the subject.

Follow your dreams, but don't quit your day job until you can support yourself.

Take notes when your boss gives you instructions. Ask him or her to slow down and repeat if you don't understand.

Don't make a big deal out of a little thing.

Everyone has his or her own view of reality. Don't take it personally when other people don't share yours.

Don't let someone else talk you into his or her version of reality if you don't agree.

Don't take things—even little things—from work. It's stealing.

Honor your company's corporate philosophy.
If you can't, look for another job.

If your boss appropriates your suggestions,
share your brightest ideas in a meeting where
others will hear that they're yours.

People who are positive and fun attract people
who are positive and fun, and they can soften
people who are grumpy.

Start each project with enthusiasm, and finish
it on time.

Even when you fail in a project, you are not
a failure. Don't let yourself think you are, or
you'll convince others, too.

When overwhelmed by too much work,
ask your boss to suggest which jobs have the
highest priorities.

If you don't have anything to do, find
something to do.

Use gender-free language: letter carrier, chair
person, flight attendant, server, and so on.

Don't tell insensitive jokes, and don't laugh
when others do.

Don't agree to work at a company where you
feel uncomfortable with the people you meet
or the things you see and hear.

Don't spend more time and energy making a
decision than it's worth.

Don't waste your time over-analyzing whether
the decision you made was right.

Write thank-you notes after job interviews, and be sure to get the interviewer's name and title right.

Job interviewers like applicants with ambition, enthusiasm, and confidence.

Keep a couple of samples of your work, letters from satisfied customers, performance appraisals, and letters of commendation *away from work*, just in case.

For managers: Management that is indifferent to the concerns of employees will have employees who are indifferent to the concerns of management.

Honesty isn't the best policy if you feel your boss is a jerk.

Think of your job as a game. There are strategies that can lead to success and traps that can cost you. Take time to learn the rules.

Remember some of the positive aspects of your job each day on your way to and from work.

Generally, people believe about you what you believe about yourself.

Don't let authoritarian coworkers and bosses trigger old parent-child or sibling emotions. Learn to detach what's happening in the present from what happened in the past.

Never say anything negative at a job interview. Not about your last job, your last employer, your commute to the interview, or even your dog. Questions that try to draw negative answers from you are a test.

Be nice to everyone. Today's administrative assistant could be tomorrow's leader. Besides, it's good karma.

When you look for the best in people, that's often what you get. The opposite is true, too.

Know which tasks your boss feels are most important. Do these with care and high visibility.

Share information, but don't share all your sources.

Carrying a grudge at work is like carrying a sack of hand grenades: unproductive and potentially dangerous.

Take time from doing to think—but if your employer pays you only to *do*, it might be better to think on your own time.

Five tips for presenting information:

⚜ Know who the decision maker is.

⚜ Know what you want the decision maker to think, feel, and do after your presentation.

⚜ Determine what information you need to present to make that happen.

⚜ Use eye contact with key players.

⚜ Practice, out loud, so you can look and feel comfortable.

Date documents and drafts.

Work off stress with 20 minutes of physical exercise.

Don't assume that if your boss doesn't complain about something, he or she doesn't notice or mind.

Know the customs of your foreign coworkers and customers, and be sensitive to their preferences.

Leave your gum at home.

Pass along helpful information. Don't hoard information as a means of control.

Give someone the benefit of the doubt twice; then be suspicious.

When you've found the perfect solution to a problem, keep looking until you've found a few more. Choosing one from several gives you a greater opportunity for success.

Good ideas are often vetoed because they conflict with politics your boss is part of. Don't get angry. Learn about your offices' politics so you can avoid traps.

People are promoted for two reasons: because they appear to have good job skills or because it appears they will fit in. Sometimes, the second reason is the most important.

Look for ways to save your manager and your company time and money. Run any great ideas past your boss before you implement them.

Volunteer to do jobs you don't mind doing anyway.

Identify your weaknesses. Work on correcting them, and don't talk about it while you do.

Success comes from working smart, not hard. Prioritize your tasks; pay attention to what you're doing so you don't make mistakes; don't waste time at work doing things that aren't job-related or that make your job more complex than it needs to be.

Inner power comes from being kind to others, not controlling them.

Accept it: No job is perfect all the time.

When someone makes a rude comment, calmly say, "Excuse me, would you repeat that please?" Give him or her a chance to rethink.

At most companies, if you're not willing to be part of the solution, you're part of the problem.

Listen to music on the way to work and back home instead of news.

Rehearse difficult situations. Prepare for difficult questions and objections, and practice answering them.

Don't get hooked on proving you're a hard worker by passing up coffee breaks. Bosses usually don't notice, and it actually reduces your productivity.

Four tips for managers:

- ❋ Train and empower your staff to satisfy customers.

- ❋ Call your place of business on the phone. How does the responder sound? Call your customer service number. Make sure people aren't likely to hang up out of frustration.

- ❋ Attempt to navigate your website. Are instructions clear? Is navigation easy? Is the information accurate and complete? Is it easy for the customer to buy? Is it easy to find someone to help or answer questions?

- ❋ Don't be tempted to solve your employees' problems. Instead, learn to ask questions that will guide them to discovering answers. Notice the tone you use to ask questions. Don't sound as if you have the answers and are waiting for a dummy to catch up.

If it's your job to criticize someone, be kind. Be specific, and do it in private.

Protect yourself by telling others your deadline for supplies or information is a day or two before it really is. But don't pad your deadlines excessively.

Network now. Once you need those contacts, it's too late to start.

Go to work on days when you're just a little bit sick. Save a few sick days to take when you're well enough to enjoy them.

Get in a habit of saving your computer work regularly.

Don't take telephone calls you can postpone when you're working on a deadline.

Job security comes not only from doing your job well, but from helping your boss achieve her goals, too.

Don't skip breakfast.
Don't skip lunch.
Don't skip an opportunity to be calm.

Remember that if you don't ask for what you want, you'll get what others want to give you.

Visualize the results you want, not the ones you fear.

People tend to remember the first and last blocks of information in a series and forget what's in the middle. Take breaks when you're learning new material so you create firsts and lasts. Write memos with three or fewer points.

You won't get everything you ask for. Don't take it personally. Don't stop asking.

Be flexible.

Try to keep your work life and your home life separate.

If it seems too good to be true, it probably is.

Misery loves company, and if you listen to others' problems too often or too long, you'll be miserable, too.

Be a problem solver.

Four more tips for presenting information:

- ✳ Introduce your point.

- ✳ Give your facts.

- ✳ Draw your conclusion.

- ✳ Ask for action.

When a coworker expects you to be impressed and you're not, be polite and say something nonspecific, like, "Amazing," or "Wow, what a story!"

When you feel you absolutely must take action, stop. Wait until the urgency to act has passed. After a while, if you still believe taking action is right, then do it.

Don't be pressured into signing rosters for information or training you didn't receive.

Only people who don't do anything don't make any mistakes.

Your body language and your tone of voice often say more than your words.

From time to time, ask a trusted work friend to let you know what kind of impression you're making.

Try not to smoke before a job interview. If you must, try to smoke in open air and use a breath freshener.

Read a different magazine each week just to see what's out there.

Go out of your way to make the new person feel welcome. It will make you both feel good, and you can't have too many allies.

No one can give you authority. But if you act like you have it, others will believe you do.

People with high confidence and low skills are given more recognition and opportunities to advance than people with low confidence and high skills.

Ask permission from your telephone caller before putting him or her on hold.

Stack your to-do pile in order: the task you want to do first on top, the next under that, and so on.

When you tell your boss about a problem, have a few solutions to suggest.

If you want to know what you believe, look at what you've created in your life.

Often, being a good listener will get you further than being a good talker.

Don't spend time with people who whine. (Don't whine yourself.)

You don't have to like everyone you have lunch with. Lunches with people who can share important information are as important as lunches with people you enjoy.

Work is an important part of your life, but it's only part of it. Be sure to also include friends, fun, giving, and spiritual growth.

Bosses are moody.
Coworkers are moody.
When you're moody, try not to take it out on your boss and coworkers.

Practice taking criticism gracefully. Ask yourself, *What can I learn from this?*

Ignore trivial things you can't control. If you can't ignore them, at least keep quiet about them.

Don't fight to win the battle if it means you'll lose the war.

Treat the boss like a good guy—even if he or she isn't.

Notice what time of the day you're most energetic and enthusiastic. Try to do your most demanding work then.

Generally, good work is taken for granted and only the errors will be mentioned. Don't wait for applause from your boss to feel good. Find reasons to feel good about yourself yourself.

Sometimes it takes years for a good idea to be recognized for the gem it is. Don't give up.

For management: When company earnings are up, employee earnings should be raised, too.

A trick to help you remember the order of points in a talk is to mentally assign a point to each finger. As you speak, keep your place by resting the corresponding finger on the lectern, the table, or your lap.

Tell a story once, twice if you must, and then retire it.

Speakers' rule for successful talks:

* Tell 'em what you're going to tell 'em.
* Tell 'em.
* Tell 'em what you told 'em.

Have fun at work every day. You spend more time at work than anyplace else, so you should try to enjoy it.

Bring flowers or pictures of your family to your work area. This is your home-away-from-home—do what you can to make it pleasant.

Bring your favorite foods to snack on. Don't trust the local deli and don't plan to do without. (When desperate, you'll eat *anything!*)

Here are four types of people, and how to win them over:

- ※ *Directors* like to be in charge. Give them facts quickly and clearly. Let them know what to expect.

- ※ *Promoters* like to gather information and pass it along. Help them find ways to solve problems and overcome challenges.

- ※ *Analyzers* like to question and analyze issues from all sides. Don't ask them to be promoters.

- ※ *Supporters* like to support others. Let them know you appreciate their help.

You will usually be your own worst enemy. Look for ways you might be sabotaging yourself.

Often, we read what we think is there, and we don't see misspelled words or words that are wrong or missing. Proofread your message, word by word. Out loud, if you can. Read slowly. Make sure you've actually written what you think you have.

People won't always do what you want them to, but if they like you, they'll go along most of the time.

Notice how your boss prefers to get information, and use that style. Some prefer to hear only the bottom line; others want to chat first. When in doubt, ask the secretary. If you can't do that, ask your boss.

People don't resent things they have to do. They resent doing things they weren't honest enough to say they didn't want to do.

Listen a lot. Smile a lot. Forgive a lot.

Be quick to forgive and slow to judge.

You can hide from office politics, but you can't escape them. Learning how they work at your job can make the difference between sweet success and sudden death.

When you're telling a story and your listener interrupts with, "You already told me that," take the hint.

Be polite to your customers or clients; don't treat them like the next chore you have to do. Take the time to ask complete sentences. Instead of, "Name?" Ask, "What's your name?" Don't just say, "Here for…?" Ask, "What are you here for?"

Don't tell everyone how people did things at your old company. Unless you were hired to make changes, wait until you prove yourself before you suggest new procedures.

Talk to a financial advisor even if you don't think you have much money. What you earn won't determine your financial future as much as what you do with what you earn.

Welcome the unexpected. It will come anyway, and the more positive you are about it, the more successful you'll be at handling it.

Something you do with passion is more likely to succeed than something you do out of duty.

If you don't like being a team player, don't take a job where that's an important part of your work.

When someone comes to you with a problem ask, "What do you think might work?"

Need to be intuitive? Creative? Cover your left nostril and breathe through your right.

Need to be logical? Cover your right nostril and breathe through the left.

Good employees are not necessarily good supervisors. If you are promoted, get training—at your company or outside—for the role.

When negotiating a salary or asking for a raise, ask for more than you expect. You can always come down, but you can never go up.

Learn the difference between a problem and an inconvenience.

Work is not a democracy, so your vote on how to do things may not matter very much. Let that be okay, or find another job.

Remember to say, "please," and, "thank you."

Three steps to success:

- Identify a skill you admire.

- Find out what you can do to learn it.

- Do what it takes to get it.

Work isn't the place to brag about your sexual conquests. Work isn't really the place to brag about anything.

Look for others' hidden agendas. It's okay for them to be there, but it's to your benefit to know what they are.
Be sure you know what yours are, too.

Practice harmlessness.

It's human nature to want to edit, rewrite, or change what others write. Try not to take it personally.

People ask for advice when they don't want to do what they know they should do. Be sympathetic, and let them figure it out for themselves.

Be nice to secretaries and assistants. Most have information you don't have. Some will hint or tell you about it. All have their boss's ear.

Make yourself indispensible, unless you want a promotion. Then, make yourself promotable by sharing information so someone else can take your place.

If it's your job to write business reports, get training. Get a book, or take a class, and learn how to write them well.

Don't put words into someone else's mouth. Don't let someone else put words into your mouth.

Don't apologize unless it's your fault. Saying, "I'm sorry," when someone is upset can link you to the problem, even if you weren't involved.

Post these tips where you will see them regularly:

- Slow down. This is your life! You need to have fun!
- Relax. Don't take everything seriously.
- Remember to play. And laugh.
- Learn the difference between needing and wanting.
- Reevaluate your life frequently. Is it working?
- Reevaluate your goals. Are they the right ones?
- Take care of yourself first.
- Say no. You probably don't have to do a lot of the things you think you have to do.

When you have the right job, you don't have to struggle to succeed.

In the scramble to do and have, it's easy to forget to *be*—to be gentle with yourself and others, to be pleased with small successes, to be happy in the moment.

You'll probably forget a lot of this. Read the book again.